Backyard Animals
Squirrels

Lauren Diemer

Weigl Publishers Inc.

Published by Weigl Publishers Inc.
350 5th Avenue, Suite 3304, PMB 6G
New York, NY 10118-0069
Website: www.weigl.com

Library of Congress Cataloging-in-Publication Data

Diemer, Lauren.
  Squirrels / Lauren Diemer.
      p. cm. -- (Backyard animals)
  ISBN 978-1-59036-671-4 (hard cover : alk. paper) -- ISBN 978-1-59036-672-1 (soft
cover : alk. paper)
  1. Squirrels--Juvenile literature. I. Title.
  QL737.R68D54 2008
  599.36--dc22

                                      2006102029

Printed in the United States of America
1 2 3 4 5 6 7 8 9 0 11 10 09 08 07

Editor Heather C. Hudak
Design and Layout Terry Paulhus

Cover: Squirrels live alone. It is rare to see a group of squirrels.

Contents

Meet the Squirrel

Squirrels are small, common **rodents**. They are **mammals** that have a bushy tail.

There are three main **species** of squirrels. These are tree squirrels, ground squirrels, and flying squirrels. Ground and tree squirrels are most active during the day. Flying squirrels are nocturnal. This means they are most active at night.

Squirrels live on every part of the world except Australia and Antarctica. They live in forests, deserts, prairie regions, and mountain areas. Many squirrels live in towns and cities. They often can be found in nature near people.

Fascinating Facts

Squirrels communicate in many ways. Sometimes, they make high-pitched sounds. They may flick their tail to scare away **predators**.

In the summer, squirrels are most active during sunrise and sunset.

All about Squirrels

There are about 230 different species of tree and ground squirrels. Flying squirrels have about 43 species.

Squirrels come in many different colors and sizes. Their fur can be black, brown, red, or gray. In Africa, there are pygmy squirrels that are only 5 inches (13 centimeters) long. In Asia, Indian giant squirrels are about 36 inches (91 cm) long.

One of the most common squirrel species in North America is the red squirrel. Red squirrels often live in the northern United States and Canada. The eastern fox squirrel, the gray squirrel, and the 13-lined ground squirrel also are common in North America.

Fascinating Facts

Chipmunks, marmots, and prairie dogs are related to squirrels.

Types of Squirrels

Flying Squirrel

- Does not hibernate, or spend the winter sleeping
- Has flaps of skin along its sides for gliding through the air
- Can glide up to 150 feet (46 meters)

Ground Squirrel

- Most hibernate; some estivate, or sleep through hot summer weather

Tree Squirrel

- Makes dreys, or nests of leaves, in the hollows of trees
- Does not hibernate

Squirrel History

Fossils of tree squirrels in North America date back 30 to 40 million years. However, scientists believe that tree squirrels lived earlier. The oldest fossils of ground squirrels are 12 million years old.

Many squirrels have **adapted** to living near people. Still, some species have suffered because of human activity. In the 1800s and 1900s, the number of Delmarva fox squirrels decreased. This is because the forests where they lived were cleared for farming. In the United States, the fox squirrel was listed as **endangered** in the 1960s. A program was set up to restore its numbers.

Fascinating Facts

The word *squirrel* comes from the Greek words *skia*, which means "shadow," and *oura*, which means "tail." Squirrels were given this name because they sit in the shadow of their tail.

The fox squirrel is the biggest type of tree squirrel. It can reach 2 feet (61 cm) long and weigh 1 to 3 pounds (0.5 to 1.4 kilograms).

Squirrel Shelter

A squirrel will claim a piece of land as its own. This space is called the squirrel's range. Some squirrels will build their homes here and try to keep other squirrels from living in the area. Other squirrels may share this range.

Tree squirrels live in trees. Many of their predators cannot climb trees. Tree squirrels make dreys from twigs and bark. The dreys are lined with fur, feathers, moss, grass, or dead leaves.

Ground squirrels live in burrows underground. They may live in rotting logs, in gaps under buildings, or in other protected places.

Tree squirrels build dreys between strong branches.

Some tree squirrels will make their home in woodpecker holes.

Squirrel Features

Squirrels are adapted for living in nature. In the winter, a thick coat of fluffy fur keeps squirrels warm by trapping a layer of air close to their body. Other parts of a squirrel's body have special features and uses, too.

NOSE
Squirrels have a keen sense of smell. This helps them find food.

EYES
Squirrels have large eyes on the sides of their head. This helps them see all around. Squirrels have excellent vision. Flying squirrels can see in the dark.

TEETH
All squirrels have sharp front teeth. They use their teeth to break open nuts to eat. Their teeth can be used to fend off predators, such as eagles, foxes, wild cats, and snakes.

TAIL

In the rain, a squirrel will use its tail as an umbrella. On cold days, squirrels use their tail as a blanket. A squirrel's tail can help balance the animal while climbing trees. If the squirrel falls from a tree, its tail acts as a parachute. The tail will cushion the fall.

CLAWS

Squirrels have sharp claws. They use their claws for climbing trees.

What Do Squirrels Eat?

Squirrels are **omnivores**. They eat nuts, seeds, berries, mushrooms, and green vegetation. Sometimes, they eat insects, eggs, and small animals, such as lizards and frogs. Squirrels may eat from bird feeders.

Most squirrels store food. Ground squirrels have pouches in their cheeks. They use these pouches to carry food to their burrows for storage. Tree squirrels bury food in the ground, in hollow trees, or under leaves.

Most ground squirrels hibernate in winter. To prepare for winter, they eat more food in autumn. This increases their body fat. They live on the fat during the cold months. Some squirrels do not have enough body fat to sleep through the winter. They wake up every few days to eat. These squirrels store food to eat during the cold months.

Fascinating Facts

Squirrels spend a great deal of time licking their fur. They groom with their paws to keep the fur clean.

Sometimes squirrels do not collect all of the nuts they have buried. These nuts grow into trees.

Squirrel Life Cycle

Male and female squirrels mate in early spring. The female will give birth about 4 to 6 weeks later. She will build a home for her babies. Depending on the type of squirrel, the babies will be born in a burrow or a drey.

Birth

Squirrel babies cannot see when they are born. They are hairless, and they have no teeth. The babies drink milk from their mother. The mother squirrel will not allow others near her babies. Not even the father can come close.

3 to 7 Weeks Old

At 3 weeks, the babies have two teeth and some hair on their back. By 5 weeks, their ears and eyes are open. Squirrel babies begin eating more than just their mother's milk at 7 weeks. They leave the nest to explore. At this age, the babies are covered in hair. They are about half the size of an adult squirrel.

Tree squirrels have three to five babies in a **litter**. Ground squirrels have 3 to 10 babies. Squirrels live about five years. Some live as long as 15 years.

10 to 12 Weeks Old

By 10 to 12 weeks of age, young squirrels eat the same food as their mother. They stop drinking her milk. The babies leave their mother and begin to care for themselves.

By the fall, the squirrels build homes of their own. They collect and store food for winter. In the spring, they will mate and have babies.

Encountering Squirrels

Sometimes a squirrel may be injured or orphaned. It is important not to touch the animal. Squirrels have sharp teeth, and they may bite. They carry diseases that can make people ill. Tell an adult about the injured animal. Then, talk to a veterinarian about how to help the squirrel.

Squirrels do not make good pets. They cannot be house trained. A baby squirrel should not be raised by people and then released into nature. The squirrel will not have the skills it needs to survive, such as building a home or searching for food.

Useful Websites

For more information about squirrels and tips about how to care for an injured or orphaned squirrel, visit **www.squirrels.org**

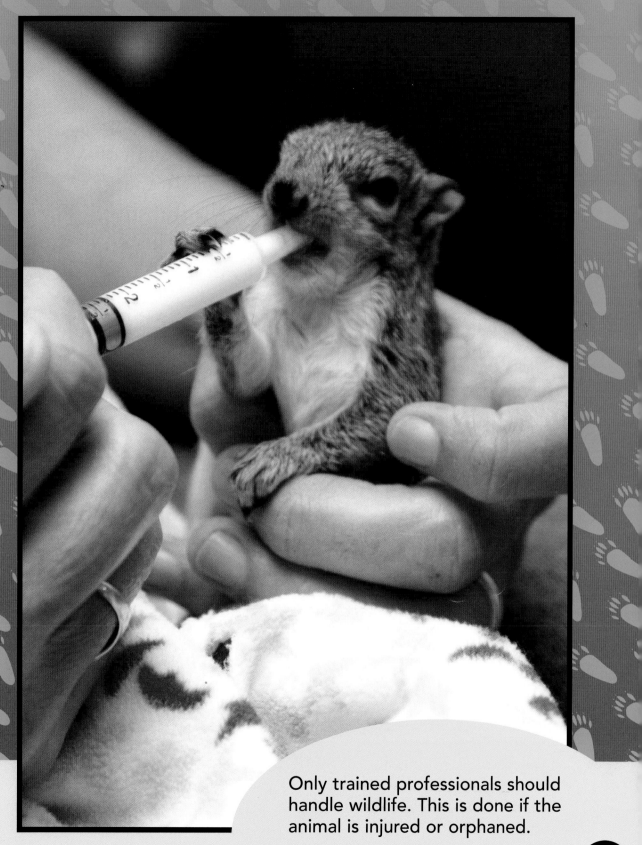

Only trained professionals should handle wildlife. This is done if the animal is injured or orphaned.

Myths and Legends

People in all parts of the world tell stories about squirrels. In Scandinavia, the squirrel is a symbol of bad luck. In Great Britain, the squirrel's energy was thought to help gardens grow. The British brought squirrels from other countries to help their gardens look better.

Cherokee Indians believed that eating squirrels would cause **arthritis**. This is because squirrels look like they have poor posture. They actually have a flexible spine.

Some American Indian groups believed that eating squirrels would cause their crops to die.

Squirrel's Song

Here is a version of a Hopi Indian tale.

Every day, Squirrel and Chipmunk stole peaches from the old Hopi man's orchard. Then, they then sat in the Sun and ate.

One day, Squirrel and Chipmunk decided to sing and dance after they had finished eating. The Hopi man heard their singing. He began to chase Squirrel and Chipmunk. They ran to Squirrel's house to hide, but the Hopi man waited outside.

Chipmunk and Squirrel laughed at the man because he could not catch them. Chipmunk decided to leave Squirrel's house. He ran so fast that the Hopi man could not catch him.

After that, Squirrel and Chipmunk did not fear the Hopi man. This is why squirrels and chipmunks today still eat the Hopi peoples' peaches and destroy their orchards. If the Hopi man had caught them, they would have stopped.

Frequently Asked Questions

How do flying squirrels glide?

Answer: A furry flap of loose skin connects a flying squirrel's front and back legs. The flap forms a kind of parachute. The squirrel glides from higher branches to lower branches with its legs spread wide apart.

What does a ground squirrel's burrow look like?

Answer: A burrow often has a sleeping chamber, a winter chamber, and two entrances. The squirrel cannot be trapped below if one entrance is blocked by predators, dirt, or snow.

How can squirrels run along wires easily?

Answer: Squirrels have sharp claws for gripping. Their tails help them balance when they walk along branches or wires.

Puzzler

See if you can answer these questions about squirrels.

1. Name two uses for a squirrel's tail.
2. When are flying squirrels most active?
3. What are the three main groups of squirrels?
4. Which type of squirrel carries food in the pouches of its cheeks?
5. How long do squirrels live?

Answers: 1. to balance the squirrel, as a parachute, as a cushion, as a blanket, and to protect it from rain 2. at night 3. tree squirrels, flying squirrels, and ground squirrels 4. ground squirrels 5. between 5 and 15 years

Find Out More

There are many more interesting facts to learn about squirrels. To learn more, take a look at these books.

Swanson, Diane. *Welcome to the World of Squirrels.* Walrus Books, 2001.

Thorington, Richard W., Jr., and Katie E. Ferrell. *Squirrels: The Animal Answer Guide.* The Johns Hopkins University Press, 2006.

Words to Know

adapted: adjusted to the natural environment

arthritis: painful swelling and stiffness of the joints

endangered: to be at risk of disappearing

fossils: the hardened remains of a plant or animal that lived long ago

litter: a group of animals that is born to one mother at the same time

mammals: animals that have warm blood and feed milk to their young

omnivores: animals that eat plants and other animals

predators: animals that hunt other animals for food

rodents: small animals with sharp front teeth that do not stop growing

species: a group of animals that share specific features

Index